Crop Circles of 1991
A pictorial record

Busty Taylor

Beckhampton

Published by:
Beckhampton Books
The Lamb Yard, The Parade, Marlborough, Wiltshire
Tel: 0672 515054

Publisher: Sir Rupert Mackeson Bart MA
© Text - Brian Grist
© Photographs - Busty Taylor/George Wingfield
© This edition - Beckhampton Books

Wholesalers:
Marlborough Books Wholesalers
6 Milton Road, Swindon, Wiltshire
Tel: 0793 432787 Fax: 0793 421640

Shop Retail from:
All good bookshops including
W H Smith, Waterstones, Dillons, Hatchards, etc.

Mail Order Retail from:
Specialist Knowledge Services
20 Paul Street, Frome, Somerset
Tel: 0373 451777

Acknowledgments: Busty wishes to express his special thanks to the following for their help and support: Cathy and Nigel Taylor, Mrs. Pat Pirriy, Omar Fowler, Pat Delgado, Colin Andrews, Dr. Terence Meaden, David Tilt, Richard Andrews, George Wingfield, Brian Grist, and fellow council members of the Centre for Crop Circle Studies (CCCS). At Beckhampton Books he wishes to thank Ron Stephens for typesetting and design, Sarah Chidgey for editorial help, Pat Turner for production help, and Eamonn Mullane for proof reading.

ISBN: 1 874560 00 5

INTRODUCTION
by Brian Grist

This book is devoted entirely to photographs of one season's crop circle formations and is the first of what will hopefully develop into a series of volumes concerning one of the most enduring and compelling enigmas of the contemporary world. In this case, the featured season is 1991 and what is presented here is a selection of some of the most striking images that appeared in the fields that summer. All bar one of the photographs were taken by Busty Taylor; the exception being that of the 'Mandlebrot' complex at Ickleton (p.48), which appears here courtesy of George Wingfield.

Busty Taylor's involvement with crop circles dates back to August 3rd, 1985, when he spotted a set of five symmetrically arranged circles (a 'quintuplet') in a field of corn whilst piloting a light aeroplane over Goodworth Clatford, near Andover. Since then, Busty has discovered and photographed more crop circles than any other single person. A founder member of CPR (Circles Phenomenon Research) and CCCS (Centre for Crop Circle Studies), Busty has worked alongside most if not all of the most prominent researchers and has lectured far and wide, including the United States, on the subject.

There can be no doubt that Busty's reputation as the foremost photographer of crop circles is fully justified. In achieving this status, he has found himself able to combine and make creative use of his passions for both flying and taking pictures. His aerial shots, taken from the cockpit, are certainly the best known of the phenomenon and have greatly stimulated interest and recognition. Busty pioneered the highly successful method of photographing crop circles with a camera on a 20ft long aluminium rod; he now works with rods of up to 40ft.

This book makes no pretence towards being anything other than a collection of photographs and, as such, is not the place to enter into the long-standing debate concerning the origin of the cropworks depicted herein. It would, however, be remiss of us to avoid pointing out that a number of them were probably man-made and that opinion remains divided as to whether or not they all were. Of one thing we can nevertheless be certain: that, regardless of whoever or whatever created these intriguing designs in the landscape, Busty Taylor deserves applause for his prowess in a craft which succeeds in preserving, albeit on film, images that are otherwise destined to perish in the annual harvest.

Note: Busty's aerial shots are indicated (A) pole-shots (P) and those taken with a hand-held camera (H).

Crop circles tend to cluster in the same locations, hence the reader finds in the book different formations with the same title.

4

Photographs June 14th/July 2nd

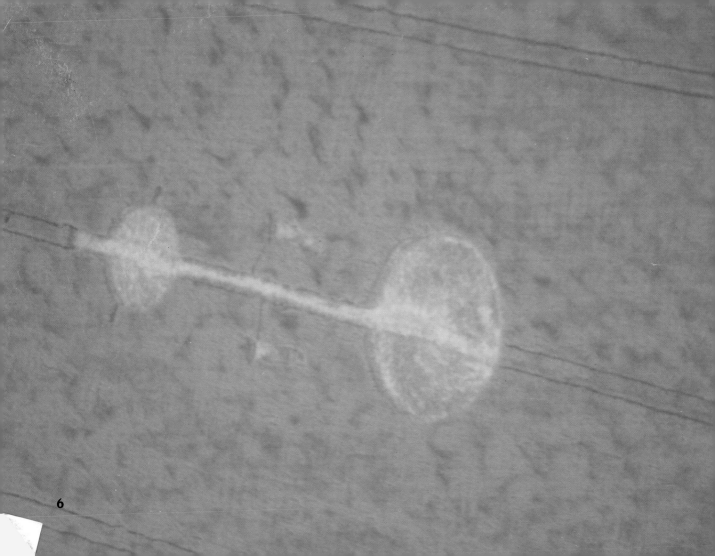

6

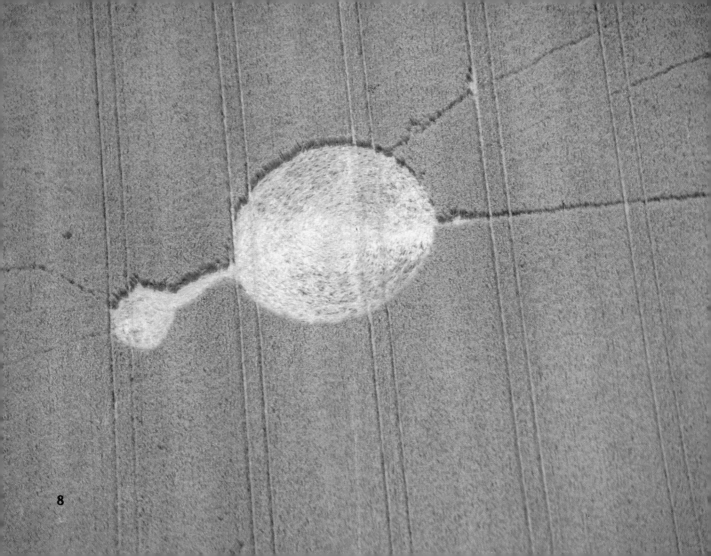

8

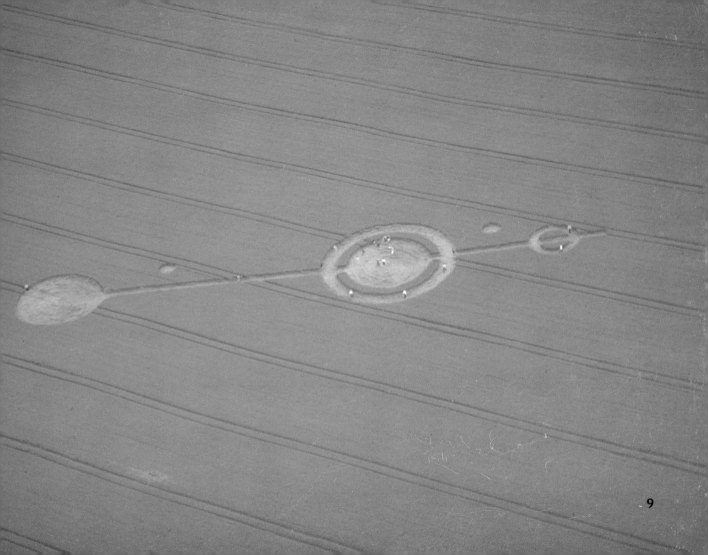

9

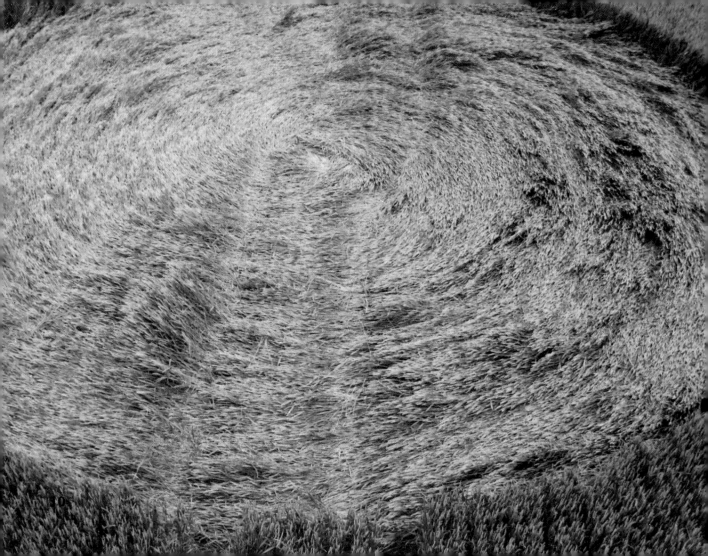

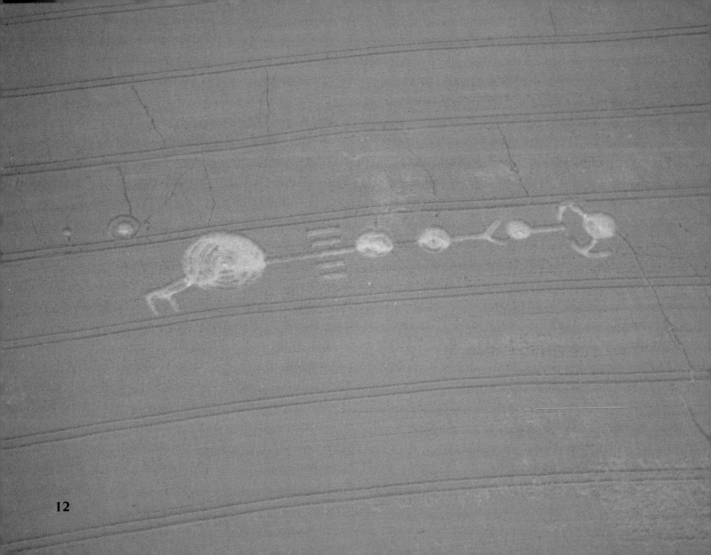

12

Photographs July 3rd/19th

14

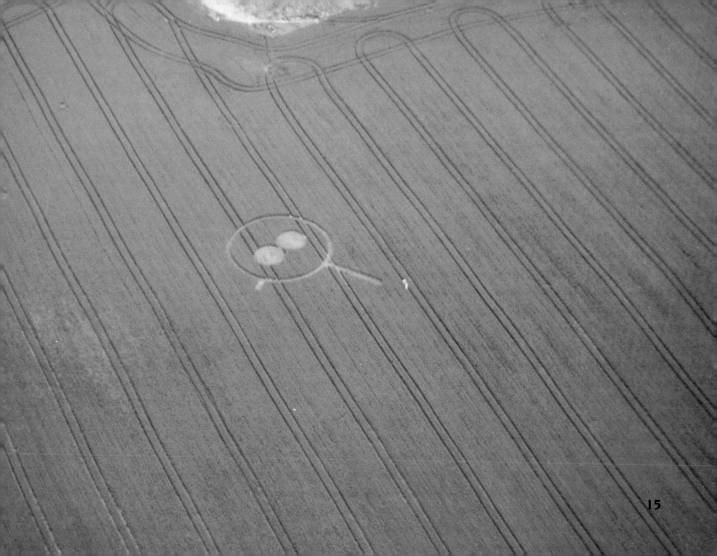

15

16

18

20

21

22

Photographs July 20th/26th

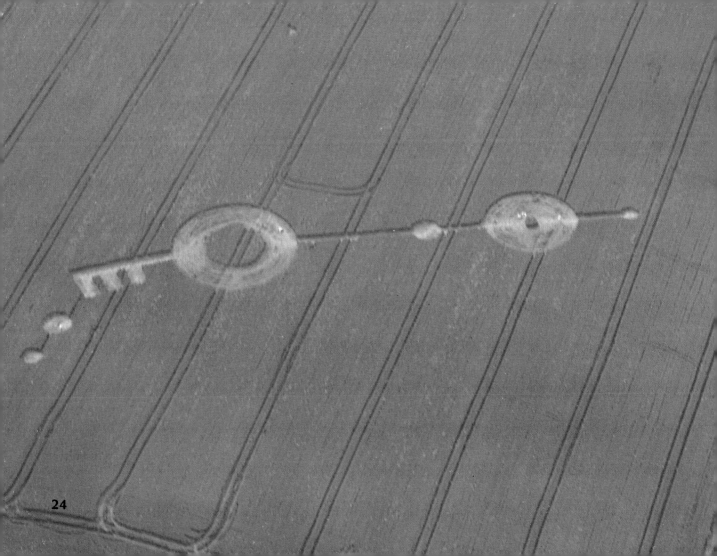

24

30

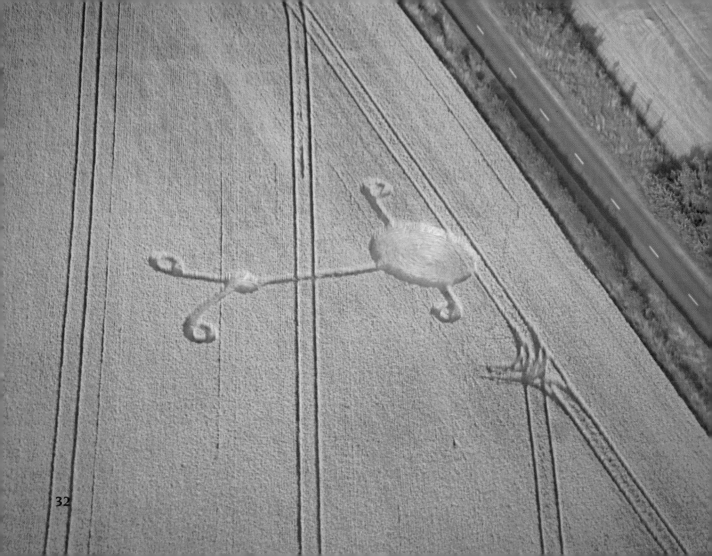

32

Photographs July 27th/August 3rd

38

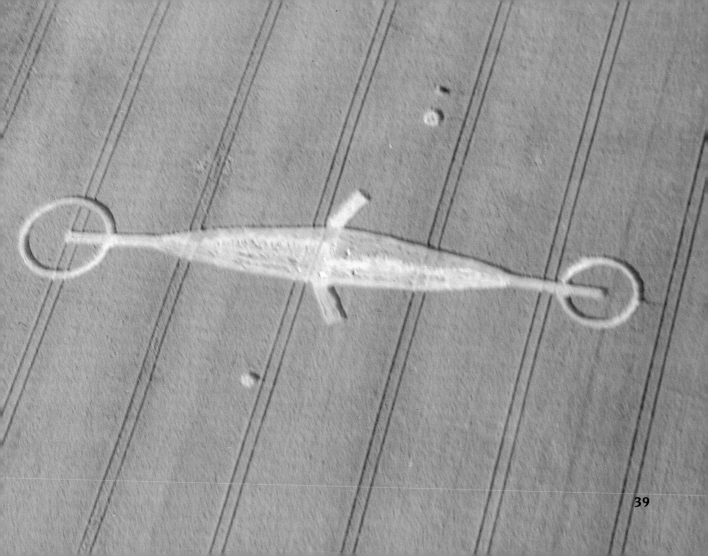

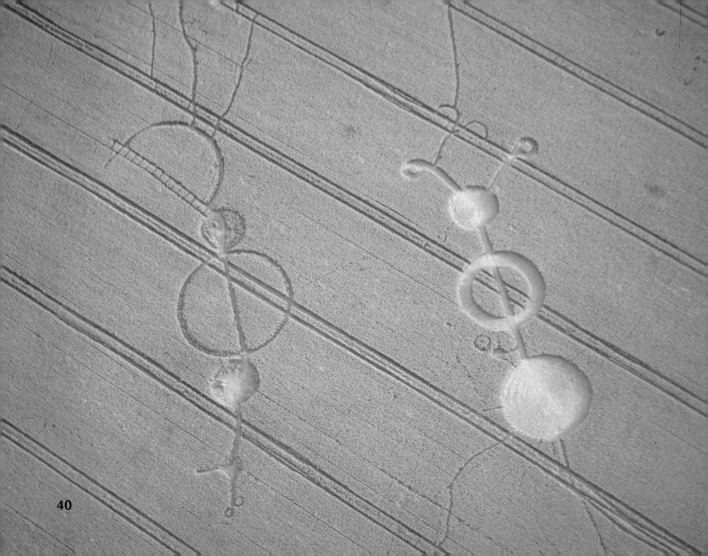

40

41

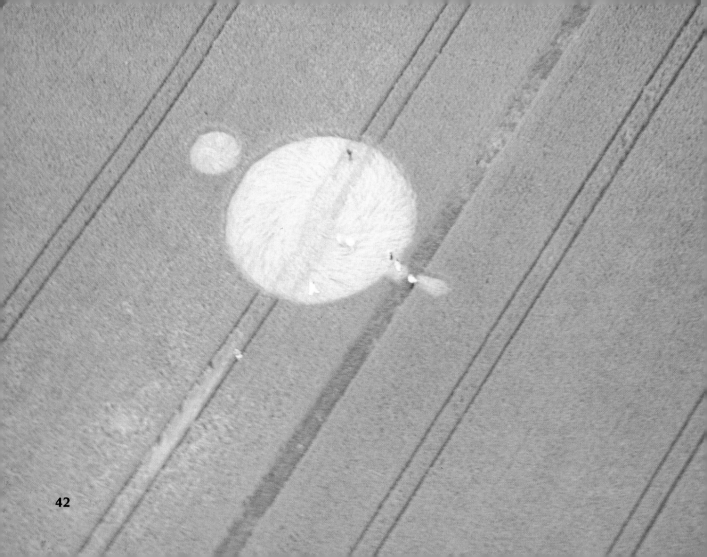

42

Photographs August 4th/15th

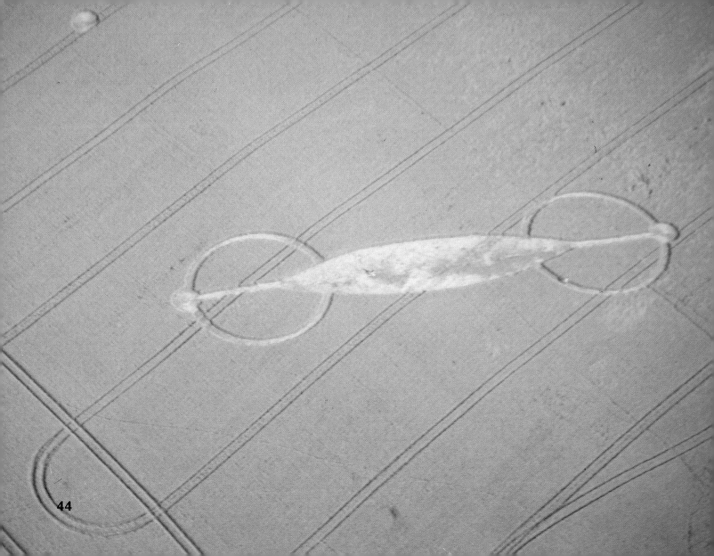

44

46

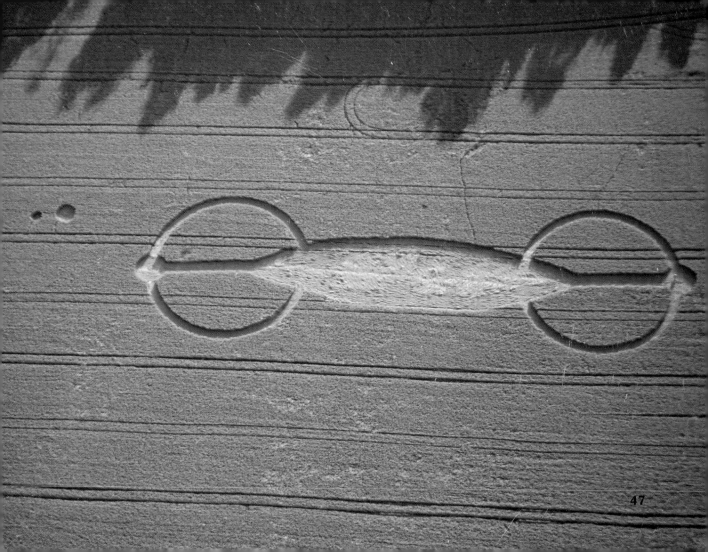

47

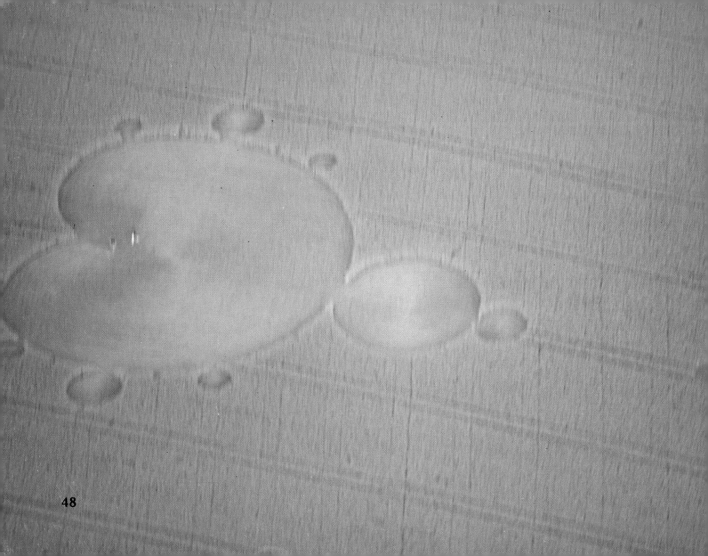